NATIONAL COOPERATIVE TRANSIT RESEARCH & DEVELOPMENT PROGRAM

# 11 Synthesis of Transit Practice

# Traffic Control and Regulation at Transit Stops

**WOODROW W. RANKIN**
**Bethesda, Maryland**

*Topic Panel*

FRANK E. BARKER, *Chicago Transit Authority*
BENJAMIN H. COTTRELL, JR., *Virginia Highway & Transportation Research Council*
JOHN A. DRAYSON, *D.C. Department of Transportation*
DAVID K. WITHEFORD, *Transportation Research Board*
PETER WOOD, *The MITRE Corporation*
CHARLES E. ZELL, *Sacramento, California*
BERT ARRILLAGA, *Urban Mass Transportation Administration* (Liaison)
HOWARD H. BISSELL, *Federal Highway Administration* (Liaison)

RESEARCH SPONSORED BY THE URBAN MASS TRANSPORTATION ADMINISTRATION OF THE U.S. DEPARTMENT OF TRANSPORTATION

*Subject Area*
Operations and Traffic Control

*Modes*
Highway Transportation
Public Transit

TRANSPORTATION RESEARCH BOARD
National Research Council
Washington, D.C. July 1987

## NATIONAL COOPERATIVE TRANSIT RESEARCH & DEVELOPMENT PROGRAM

Administrators, engineers, and many others in the transit industry are faced with a multitude of complex problems that range between local, regional, and national in their prevalence. How they might be solved is open to a variety of approaches; however, it is an established fact that a highly effective approach to problems of widespread commonality is one in which operating agencies join cooperatively to support, both in financial and other participatory respects, systematic research that is well designed, practically oriented, and carried out by highly competent researchers. As problems grow rapidly in number and escalate in complexity, the value of an orderly, high-quality cooperative endeavor likewise escalates.

Recognizing this in light of the many needs of the transit industry at large, the Urban Mass Transportation Administration, U.S. Department of Transportation, got under way in 1980 the National Cooperative Transit Research & Development Program (NCTRP). This is an objective national program that provides a mechanism by which UMTA's principal client groups across the nation can join cooperatively in an attempt to solve near-term public transportation problems through applied research, development, test, and evaluation. The client groups thereby have a channel through which they can directly influence a portion of UMTA's annual activities in transit technology development and deployment. Although present funding of the NCTRP is entirely from UMTA's Section 6 funds, the planning leading to inception of the Program envisioned that UMTA's client groups would join ultimately in providing additional support, thereby enabling the Program to address a large number of problems each year.

The NCTRP operates by means of agreements between UMTA as the sponsor and (1) the National Research Council as the Primary Technical Contractor (PTC) responsible for administrative and technical services, (2) the American Public Transit Association, responsible for operation of a Technical Steering Group (TSG) comprised of representatives of transit operators, local government officials, State DOT officials, and officials from UMTA's Office of Technical Assistance, and (3) the Urban Consortium for Technology Initiatives/Public Technology, Inc., responsible for providing the local government officials for the Technical Steering Group.

Research Programs for the NCTRP are developed annually by the Technical Steering Group, which identifies key problems, ranks them in order of priority, and establishes programs of projects for UMTA approval. Once approved, they are referred to the National Research Council for acceptance and administration through the Transportation Research Board.

Research projects addressing the problems referred from UMTA are defined by panels of experts established by the Board to provide technical guidance and counsel in the problem areas. The projects are advertised widely for proposals, and qualified agencies are selected on the basis of research plans offering the greatest probabilities of success. The research is carried out by these agencies under contract to the National Research Council, and administration and surveillance of the contract work are the responsibilities of the National Research Council and Board.

The needs for transit research are many, and the National Cooperative Transit Research & Development Program is a mechanism for deriving timely solutions for transportation problems of mutual concern to many responsible groups. In doing so, the Program operates complementary to, rather than as a substitute for or duplicate of, other transit research programs.



### NCTRP SYNTHESIS 11

Project 60-1 FY 1982/1983 (Topic TS-6)
ISSN 0732-1856
ISBN 0-309-04407-3
Library of Congress Catalog Card No. 86-51177

**Price: $7.20**

### NOTICE

The project that is the subject of this report was a part of the National Cooperative Transit Research & Development Program conducted by the Transportation Research Board with the approval of the Governing Board of the National Research Council. Such approval reflects the Governing Board's judgment that the program concerned is of national importance and appropriate with respect to both the purposes and resources of the National Research Council.

The members of the technical committee selected to monitor this project and to review this report were chosen for recognized scholarly competence and with due consideration for the balance of disciplines appropriate to the project. The opinions and conclusions expressed or implied are those of the research agency that performed the research, and, while they have been accepted as appropriate by the technical committee, they are not necessarily those of the Transportation Research Board, the National Research Council, or the Urban Mass Transportation Administration, U.S. Department of Transportation.

Each report is reviewed and accepted for publication by the technical committee according to procedures established and monitored by the Transportation Research Board Executive Committee and the Governing Board of the National Research Council.

The National Research Council was established by the National Academy of Sciences in 1916 to associate the broad community of science and technology with the Academy's purposes of furthering knowledge and of advising the Federal Government. The Council has become the principal operating agency of both the National Academy of Sciences and the National Academy of Engineering in the conduct of their services to the government, the public, and the scientific and engineering communities. It is administered jointly by both Academies and the Institute of Medicine. The National Academy of Engineering and the Institute of Medicine were established in 1964 and 1970, respectively, under the charter of the National Academy of Sciences.

The Transportation Research Board evolved in 1974 from the Highway Research Board, which was established in 1920. The TRB incorporates all former HRB activities and also performs additional functions under a broader scope involving all modes of transportation and the interactions of transportation with society.

#### Special Notice

The Transportation Research Board, the National Academy of Sciences, and the Urban Mass Transportation Administration (sponsor of the National Cooperative Transit Research & Development Program) do not endorse products or manufacturers. Trade or manufacturers' names appear herein solely because they are considered essential to the clarity and completeness of project reporting.

*Published reports of the*

**NATIONAL COOPERATIVE TRANSIT RESEARCH & DEVELOPMENT PROGRAM**

*are available from:*

Transportation Research Board
National Research Council
2101 Constitution Avenue, N.W.
Washington, D.C. 20418

Printed in the United States of America

## PREFACE

A vast storehouse of information exists on nearly every subject of concern to the transit industry. Much of this information has resulted from both research and the successful application of solutions to the problems faced by practitioners in their daily work. Because previously there has been no systematic means for compiling such useful information and making it available to the entire transit community, the Urban Mass Transportation Administration of the U.S. Department of Transportation has, through the mechanism of the National Cooperative Transit Research & Development Program, authorized the Transportation Research Board to undertake a series of studies to search out and synthesize useful knowledge from all available sources and to prepare documented reports on current practices in the subject areas of concern.

This synthesis series reports on various practices, making specific recommendations where appropriate but without the detailed directions usually found in handbooks or design manuals. Nonetheless, these documents can serve similar purposes, for each is a compendium of the best knowledge available on measures found to be successful in resolving specific problems. The extent to which these reports are useful will be tempered by the user's knowledge and experience in the particular problem area.

## FOREWORD

*By Staff*
*Transportation Research Board*

**This synthesis will be of interest to traffic engineers, transit planners, and others in the highway and transit fields who are concerned with parking restrictions at bus stops. Information is presented on the regulations, signing, and markings used at bus stops.**

---

Administrators, engineers, and researchers are continually faced with problems on which much information exists, either in the form of reports or in terms of undocumented experience and practice. Unfortunately, this information often is scattered and unevaluated, and, as a consequence, in seeking solutions, full information on what has been learned about a problem frequently is not assembled. Costly research findings may go unused, valuable experience may be overlooked, and full consideration may not be given to the available methods of solving or alleviating the problem. In an effort to correct this situation, NCTRP Project 60-1, carried out by the Transportation Research Board as the research agency, has the objective of reporting on common transit problems and synthesizing available information. The synthesis reports from this endeavor constitute an NCTRP publication series in which various forms of relevant information are assembled into single, concise documents pertaining to specific problems or sets of closely related problems.

**Although there is almost always some kind of sign at a bus stop to indicate that it is a place where buses stop, there is a wide variation in the use of signs and markings**

to prohibit vehicles from parking at those stops. This report of the Transportation Research Board describes the practices used by cities to regulate parking at bus stops.

To develop this synthesis in a comprehensive manner and to ensure inclusion of significant knowledge, the Board analyzed available information assembled from numerous sources, including a large number of public transportation agencies. A topic panel of experts in the subject area was established to guide the researcher in organizing and evaluating the collected data, and to review the final synthesis report.

This synthesis is an immediately useful document that records practices that were acceptable within the limitations of the knowledge available at the time of its preparation. As the processes of advancement continue, new knowledge can be expected to be added to that now at hand.

# CONTENTS

## ACKNOWLEDGMENTS

This synthesis was completed by the Transportation Research Board under the supervision of Robert E. Skinner, Jr., Director for Special Projects. The Principal Investigators responsible for conduct of the synthesis were Thomas L. Copas and Herbert A. Pennock, Special Projects Engineers. This synthesis was edited by Anne S. Brennan.

Special appreciation is expressed to Woodrow W. Rankin, Bethesda, Maryland, who was responsible for the collection of data and the preparation of the report.

Valuable assistance in the preparation of this synthesis was provided by the Topic Panel, consisting of Frank E. Barker, Director, Street Traffic Section, Chicago Transit Authority; Benjamin H. Cottrell, Jr., Research Scientist, Virginia Highway & Transportation Research Council; John A. Drayson, Deputy Assistant Director, D.C. Department of Transportation; Peter Wood, Department Head, Transportation and Telecommunications, The MITRE Corporation; Charles E. Zell, Transportation Engineer, Sacramento, California; and Liaison Members Bert Arrillaga, Chief, Pricing and Marketing Division, Urban Mass Transportation Administration, and Howard H. Bissell, Research Engineer, Federal Highway Administration.

David K. Witheford, Engineer of Traffic and Operations, of the Transportation Research Board, assisted the Project 60-1 Staff and the Topic Panel.

Information on current practice was provieed by many transit agencies. Their cooperation and assistance were most helpful.

# TRAFFIC CONTROL AND REGULATION AT TRANSIT STOPS


## SUMMARY

This synthesis reports current practices in the regulation of traffic and the use of traffic control devices at urban on-street transit bus stops in the United States. The regulations and control devices prohibit or limit parking, standing, or stopping.

Information was collected from 137 cities with populations between 50,000 and 1,000,000. That sample included 58 percent of the cities with populations between 100,000 and 1,000,000. The information was furnished by either traffic engineering agencies or transit system operating or planning personnel.

Most of the cities (70%) have a local ordinance that prohibits either parking, stopping, or standing in a bus stop. The other cities establish parking prohibitions at bus stops with ordinances for specific locations or areas, or under provisions of general ordinances or state statutes.

Considerable variations were reported between and within cities in the extent to which parking prohibitions are believed needed and in the types of signs and curb markings used for the control. Only thirty-five percent of the cities have either No Parking signs or curb markings at all bus stops. Seven percent of the cities do not use parking prohibition signs or curb markings at bus stops. The other cities use No Parking signs, curb markings, or both, but only at selected stops.

Three types of No Parking signs and six colors or combinations of colors for curb markings were used at bus stops. Their designs usually conform to national standards. Fifty-four different use patterns of those signs and curb markings were identified. In most cities the traffic engineering agency is responsible for the installation and maintenance of those signs and markings.

More than half of city officials rated the effectiveness of the local bus stop parking controls as good, and few rated the effectiveness of their controls as poor. A consistent, good level of enforcement was identified as essential for effective bus stop parking prohibitions.

In response to perceived needs identified in the study, research is recommended on two aspects of parking controls at bus stops:

1. Additional or revised national standards for the signs and curb markings that are used for parking prohibitions, including providing more flexibility in the design standards for the combined Bus Stop Location-No Parking sign, and
2. Guidelines on when parking controls should be established at bus stops.

CHAPTER ONE

# INTRODUCTION

Uniformity in design and application is a generally accepted principle of traffic regulation and control. The *Manual on Uniform Traffic Control Devices (1)* defines that uniformity as "treating similar situations in the same way." Observations in the United States before this study, however, had shown that there apparently was no consistent practice in the use of traffic regulations and control to prohibit or limit parking at bus stops by vehicles other than buses.

The purpose of this synthesis is to review current practices for the regulation of traffic and the use of traffic control devices at on-street urban transit bus stops in the United States. Generally those regulations and control devices prohibit parking, standing, or stopping.

For the review, information on bus stop traffic regulations and control devices was collected concerning:

1. National standards and guidelines,
2. The types of regulations that are established to prohibit parking,
3. The agency responsible for initiating the regulations,
4. The types of signs and curb markings used to post those regulations,
5. The combinations of those signs and markings that are used,
6. The agency responsible for installing and maintaining the signs and curb markings, and
7. The effectiveness of local bus stop parking prohibitions as perceived by traffic engineering agencies.

The study focused on cities with populations between 50,000 and 1,000,000. Some information also was collected for cities under 50,000 and over 1,000,000, and for multi-jurisdiction transit districts.

## DEFINITIONS

In this report the term *bus stop* is used as defined in TRB Special Report 179 (*2*): "a waiting, boarding, and alighting area, usually designated by distinctive signs and by curbs or pavement markings."

The term *bus stop location sign* is used for the sign that indicates, for the information of transit patrons, the location in a bus stop where passengers normally board the bus. Information on the use and design of this sign is given in the publication *On-Street Information* (*3*).

## NATIONAL STANDARDS AND GUIDELINES FOR TRAFFIC REGULATION AND CONTROL DEVICES

### Traffic Regulation

Parking, standing, or stopping prohibitions at bus stops are traffic regulations. As such they can be established only when authorized by appropriate laws or ordinances. The Model Traffic Ordinance (MTO) (*4*) is a set of motor vehicle ordinances that are accepted as good practice. The provisions of the MTO are intended as a guide for cities to use when they develop or revise local traffic ordinances. Two sections of the MTO deal specifically with bus stop traffic regulations.

One, Section 15-5, authorizes and requires the city traffic engineer (or city engineer) to establish bus stop locations. The section requires that those bus stops be designated by appropriate signs. The other, Section 15-7, prohibits stopping, standing, or parking of vehicles other than buses in officially designated and appropriately signed bus stops. However, passenger vehicles are allowed to stop to load or unload passengers. The text of the two sections is given in Appendix A.

### Traffic Control Devices

The Manual on Uniform Traffic Control Devices (MUTCD) (*1*) has been approved by the Federal Highway Administrator as the national standard for all highways open to public travel. It covers the design and application of traffic control devices. Included in the MUTCD are general specifications for the design of two alternative Parking signs for use at bus stops, and standards and guidelines for the placement of No Parking signs and curb markings to indicate parking restrictions.

The designs of the two bus stop parking prohibition signs are discussed and illustrated in Section 2B-31 of the MUTCD. One, R7-107, has a word legend. The other, R7-107a, has a word and symbol legend. The signs are shown in Figure 1. The text of Section 2B-31 relevant to the two signs is given in Appendix B.

Section 2B-32 of the MUTCD covers the placement of urban parking signs. The text implies that signs shall be used to indicate the extent of parking regulations. The text of Section 2B-32 is given in Appendix B.

Section 3B-18 of the MUTCD covers the use of curb markings to indicate parking restrictions. At the option of local authorities, special colors (none specified) may be used for curb markings. The text specifies that signs be used with curb markings in areas where the markings are frequently covered by snow or

FIGURE 1 MUTCD bus stop parking prohibition signs.

ice. Where signs are not used (in non-snow and ice areas), the text recommends stenciling the intended meaning of the marking on the curb. The text of Section 3B-18 is given in Appendix B.

## STUDY METHODOLOGY

The principal source of information for the synthesis was two mail surveys. One, survey form A, was sent to city traffic engineers in cities with populations over 50,000. The other, survey form B, was distributed to transit system operating and planning personnel with the cooperation of the American Public Transit Association. A copy of each survey form is given in Appendix C. Survey forms were returned by traffic engineering agencies, multi-jurisdiction transit districts, and transit systems in cities with populations from 10,000 to over 1,000,000.

From the two surveys, information on the traffic regulations and control at transit stops was obtained from 137 cities with

TABLE 1

NUMBER OF CITIES USED IN DETAILED ANALYSIS

| Population Group | Survey Form Returned | | Total |
|---|---|---|---|
| | Type A | Type B | |
| 50,000 - 100,000 | 29 | 14 | 43 |
| 100,000 - 250,000 | 36 | 17 | 53 |
| 250,000 - 1,000,000 | 27 | 14 | 41 |
| All groups | 92 | 45 | 137 |

FIGURE 2 Geographic distribution of cities used in detailed analysis.

populations between 50,000 and 1,000,000. Forty-three states were represented in that group. The information from the group was used in the detailed analysis of this study. Similar information was obtained from 14 cities under 50,000, 5 cities over 1,000,000, and 28 transit districts. That information is tabulated and reported separately.

To identify whether or not city size, as measured by population, is a significant factor in the use of traffic regulations and control devices, the group of cities used in the detailed analysis was subdivided into three population groups using 1980 census data.

50,000–100,000
100,000–250,000
250,000–1,000,000

The number of cities in each population group and the type of survey form the cities received are given in Table 1. The geographical distribution of those cities is shown in Figure 2. A list of all cities and transit districts that returned completed forms is given in Appendix D.

CHAPTER TWO

# SURVEY FINDINGS

The findings reported below are based on the information supplied by the 137 cities with populations between 50,000 and 1,000,000. Information obtained for cities under 50,000, cities over 1,000,000, and the 28 transit districts is reported in less detail in a separate section.

## TRAFFIC REGULATIONS AT BUS STOPS

Ninety-six (70%) of the 137 cities have a traffic regulation similar to the provisions of the MTO that prohibits either parking, or stopping, or standing in officially designated bus stops that are appropriately signed. Generally the regulations prohibit parking, but a few prohibit stopping. With these regulations, signs or curb markings are used to indicate the parking prohibition and the length of the prohibition. The percent of cities in each population group that have a general, MTO-type ordinance prohibiting parking in bus stops is given in Table 2.

One city prohibits parking for 20 ft (6 m) on the approach side of all bus stop location signs. No other signs indicating this regulation are required. Where more than 20 ft of clear curb is required at a bus stop, the city establishes a bus zone where parking is prohibited.

Thirty-six of the 41 cities that do not have a general bus stop parking prohibition ordinance use No Parking signs or curb markings to indicate parking prohibitions in bus stops. These regulations are established with ordinances for specific locations or areas, or under a general ordinance or state statute prohibiting parking at locations where appropriate signs or curb markings are in place. The other five cities do not use parking prohibition signs or curb markings at bus stops.

### Agency Responsible for Initiating Bus Stop Traffic Control Regulations

Information on the agency that determines if parking prohibition signs or curb markings are needed at bus stops was collected from 92 cities in the 50,000 to 1,000,000 population group. They were all cities where the survey form was sent to the city traffic engineer. In 78 percent of those cities the traffic engineering agency determines if parking controls are needed at bus stops. In 17 percent of the cities those decisions are made jointly by the traffic engineering and the transit agencies. In five percent of the cities the decisions are made by the transit agency.

## TRAFFIC CONTROL DEVICES AT BUS STOPS

The purpose of bus stop parking prohibitions is to provide a length of clear curb adequate to permit buses, with a minimum

TABLE 2

USE OF GENERAL NO PARKING/BUS STOP ORDINANCE

| Population Group | Cities in Group (No.) | Cities with Ordinance (No.) | Cities with Ordinance (%) |
|---|---|---|---|
| 50,000 - 100,000 | 43 | 32 | 74 |
| 100,000 - 250,000 | 53 | 36 | 68 |
| 250,000 - 1,000,000 | 41 | 28 | 68 |
| All groups | 137 | 96 | 70 |

inconvenience to other traffic, to safely, efficiently, and conveniently load and unload passengers. Cities in the 50,000 to 1,000,000 population group reported considerable variations between and within cities in the extent to which the control is believed needed, and in the types and combinations of signs and curb markings used for the control.

Four basic concepts on the use of parking prohibitions at bus stops have been identified in this study.

1. The same types of signs and/or curb markings are used at all stops.
2. All stops have the same basic pattern of signs and/or curb markings, and supplemental signs and/or curb markings are used at selected stops.
3. Parking controls are used only as needed, and signs and/or curb markings are used only at selected stops or groups of stops.
4. Parking prohibition signs and/or curb markings are not used at bus stops.

Fifteen percent of the 137 cities follow the first concept, and 20 percent follow the second. Fifty-eight percent follow the third, and seven percent the fourth. The cities that establish parking prohibitions at bus stops reported using three types of No Parking signs and six colors, or combinations of colors, for curb markings.

The variations in the use of parking prohibition traffic control devices primarily stem from local and sometimes state policies.

- Local policies generally determine if parking prohibitions will be established at selected, all, or no bus stops.
- Local policies generally determine whether signs, curb markings, or both will be used to indicate bus stop parking prohibitions.
- Local or state policies generally influence the type of signs and curb markings used at bus stops.

Cities reported considering several factors when identifying selected stops for parking controls or stops for supplementary signs or curb markings. The demand for on-street parking in, and adjacent to, the stop was the major factor. Other factors were:

- The volume of street traffic at the stop,
- The headways of buses serving the stop, and
- The number of passengers boarding and alighting at the stop.

#### Signs at Bus Stops

A Bus Stop Location sign generally is used at all stops—either alone, in combination with a No Parking sign, or as a logo section of a combined Bus Stop Location-No Parking sign. The design of the sign or logo panel usually is unique to the bus system.

Three types of No Parking signs are used at bus stops. They are illustrated in Figure 3. When type B or C signs are used, their design usually conforms to the standards of the MUTCD. However, 20 percent of the cities using type A signs (the combined stop location and parking prohibition sign) reported that their designs for the sign are substantially different from the MUTCD standard shown in Figure 3. Some of those signs are illustrated in Figure 4. The number of cities using each type of No Parking sign is given in Table 3.

#### Curb and Pavement Markings at Bus Stops

When curb markings are used to indicate a bus stop parking prohibition, they usually are either yellow or red. However, seven cities reported using a two-color, checkered pattern. The lengths of the alternate color sections ranged from 4 to 15 ft

FIGURE 3 Types of bus stop parking prohibition signs reported in survey.

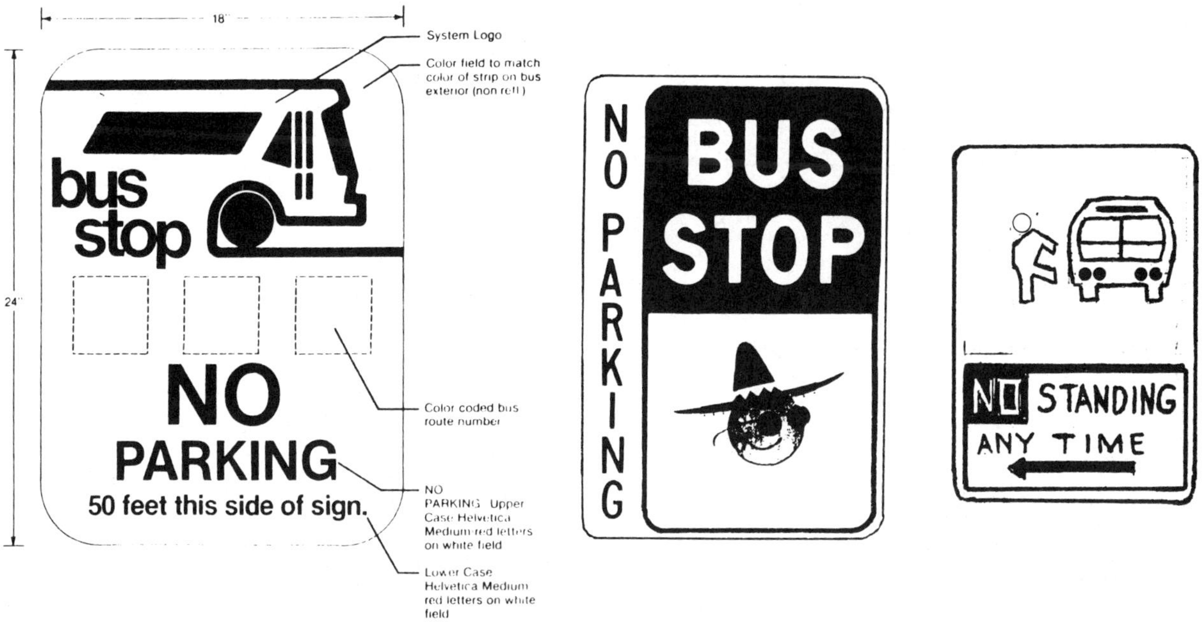


FIGURE 4 Nonstandard parking prohibition signs used at bus stops.

(1.2 to 4.6 m). Three of the cities use a red and yellow pattern. The other color combinations are: red and white, blue and white, yellow and gray, and yellow and black. A typical two-color curb marking for bus stops is illustrated in Figure 5. The number of cities using a single color or two colors for bus stop curb markings is given in Table 4.

Three cities reported using special pavement markings at bus stops. The markings are used only to indicate the limits of the bus stop in the curb lane. Signs or curb markings are used to indicate the bus stop parking prohibition. One city paints a box-end symbol in the curb lane at each end of the bus stop as shown in Figure 6. One city, as shown in Figure 6, marks the limits of bus stops where parking is prohibited with 12-in. (300-mm) wide white lines in the curb lane. The legend, BUS STOP, also is painted on the pavement. One city paints a solid white line 8 ft (2.4 m) off the curb at selected bus stops.

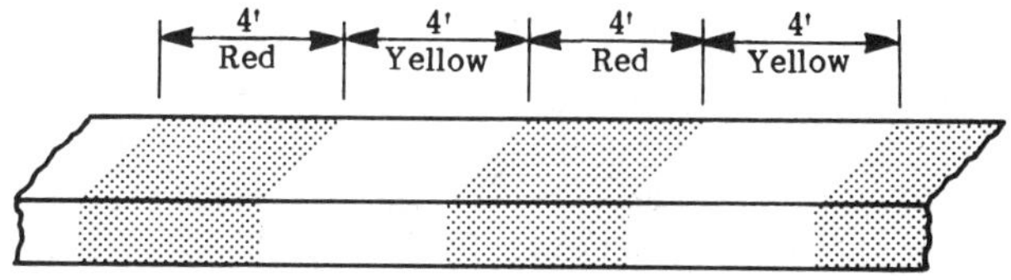


FIGURE 5 Typical two-color curb markings.

TABLE 3

NUMBER OF CITIES USING PARKING PROHIBITION SIGNS[a]

| Population Group | Type of Sign[b] | | | | No Signs |
|---|---|---|---|---|---|
| | A | B | A&B[c] | C | |
| 50,000 - 100,000 | 7 | 12 | 2 | 14 | 8 |
| 100,000 - 250,000 | 19 | 14 | 4 | 11 | 5 |
| 250,000 - 1,000,000 | 11 | 5 | 3 | 17 | 5 |
| All groups | 37 | 31 | 9 | 42 | 18 |

[a]Principal sign.

[b]As shown in Figure 3.

[c]Sign A used at some stops and Sign B at some stops.

### Patterns of Traffic Control Devices at Bus Stops

For each of the first three basic concepts on the use of parking prohibitions at bus stops, a number of patterns of No Parking signs and curb markings may be used. Fifteen were identified in this study (Table 5). The use of parking prohibition signs and curb markings with those patterns is summarized in Table 6.

For each pattern of control device use, a number of sub-patterns are possible depending on which signs, curb markings, or combination of signs and curb markings are used. A total of 54 were identified in this study. The number of cities reporting each sub-pattern and the types of signs and curb markings they use are given in Appendix E.

In half of the cities, two parking signs are used at all or selected bus stops. The usual placement of those signs at near-side, far-side, and mid-block stops is illustrated in Figure 7. The dimensions of the stops shown in the figure are typical of those reported by cities in this study. They correspond closely with the dimensions for stops used by 40-ft (12-m) buses that are given in an Institute of Transportation Engineers recommended practice for the location of bus stops (*5*). Special conditions that may require longer length stops and more signs are discussed in the recommended practice. They include:

TABLE 4

NUMBER OF CITIES USING CURB MARKINGS

| Population Group | Color | | | No Curb Markings |
|---|---|---|---|---|
| | Yellow | Red | Other[a] | |
| 50,000 - 100,000 | 16 | 6 | 2 | 19 |
| 100,000 - 250,000 | 12 | 10 | 3 | 28 |
| 250,000 - 1,000,000 | 9 | 9 | 2 | 21 |
| All groups | 37 | 25 | 7 | 68 |

[a]Two-color pattern.

- Regular use of the stop simultaneously by two or more buses,
- Use of articulated buses, and
- Regular use of handicapped passenger equipment.

### Installation and Maintenance of Signs and Curb Markings at Bus Stops

The installation and maintenance of parking prohibition signs and curb markings in the 137 cities in the 50,000 to 1,000,000 population group is usually the responsibility of either the traffic engineering or public works agency. In a few cities the transit agency shares responsibility with either traffic engineering or public works, or the transit agency is solely responsible. The agencies responsible for those functions in the 137 cities are given in Table 7. In addition, Table 7 gives the agencies responsible for the installation and maintenance of Bus Stop Location signs.

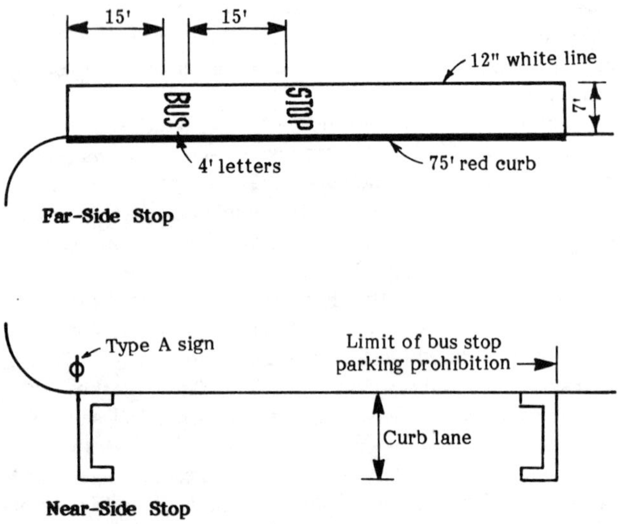


FIGURE 6 Examples of use of pavement markings at bus stops.

TABLE 5

PARKING PROHIBITION SIGN AND CURB MARKING PATTERNS AT BUS STOPS

| Pattern | Number of Cities |
|---|---|
| Concept One | |
| One sign - all stops[a] | 11 |
| Two or more signs - all stops[b] | 4 |
| One sign with curb markings - all stops[a] | 2 |
| Curb markings only - all stops | 2 |
| Concept Two | |
| One sign - all stops[a] | |
| Additional signs - selected stops[c] | 12 |
| Curb markings - selected stops | 5 |
| Additional signs and markings - selected stops[c] | 5 |
| Two or more signs - all stops[b] | |
| Curb markings - selected stops | 2 |
| Curb markings - all stops | |
| Additional signs - selected stops[a] | 4 |
| Concept Three | |
| One sign - selected stops[a] | 12 |
| Two or more signs - selected stops[b] | 20 |
| One sign with curb markings - selected stops[b] | 15 |
| Two or more signs with markings - selected stops[b] | 25 |
| Curb markings only - selected stops | 7 |
| Concept Four | |
| No signs or curb markings | 9 |

[a]Sign at bus loading point.

[b]One sign at bus loading point; second generally at start of parking prohibition.

[c]One sign generally at start of parking prohibition.

### Effectiveness of Current Bus Stop Traffic Controls

The effectiveness of the parking prohibition controls at bus stops is dependent on a number of factors. The most important one is the level of enforcement of the controls. When drivers expect little or no enforcement, illegal parking is likely to be common. When there is regular enforcement, illegal parking

TABLE 6

NUMBER OF CITIES USING PARKING PROHIBITION SIGNS AND MARKINGS AT BUS STOPS

| Signs | Curb Markings | | |
|---|---|---|---|
| | All Stops | Selected Stops | Not Used |
| All Stops | 4 | 12 | 27 |
| Selected Stops | 4 | 40 | 32 |
| Not Used | 2 | 7 | 9[a] |

[a]Stops designated by a bus stop location sign.

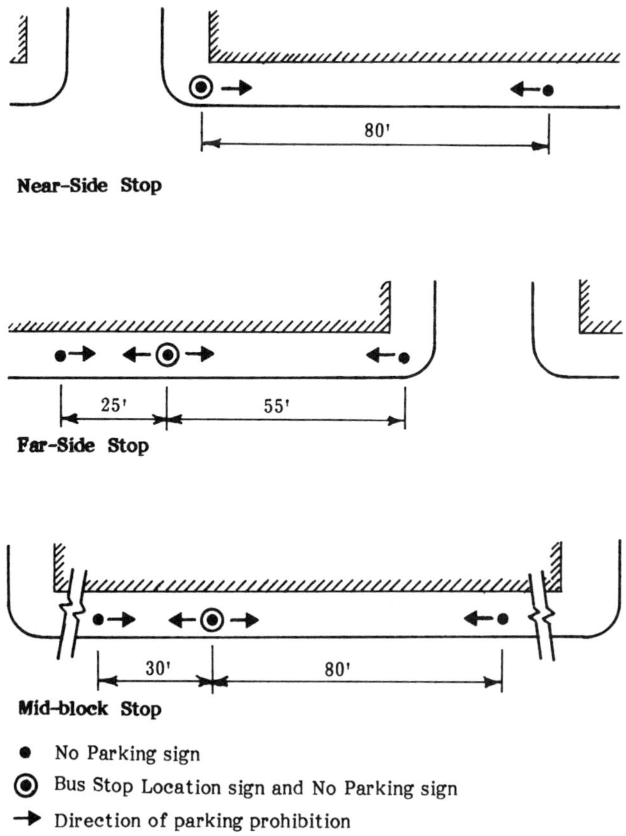


FIGURE 7 Location of No Parking signs at bus stops.

will be limited. Two cities reported that they minimize illegal parking in bus stops by having transit system employees, usually supervisors or drivers, authorized to issue citations for violations of bus stop parking regulations. Positive delineation of the bus stop parking prohibition may make it more effective. Signs and curb markings that clearly indicate the limits and length of the prohibition will make enforcement easier, and it may deter some potential violators.

The effectiveness of the bus stop parking prohibition controls is perceived as good or fair in most of the 92 cities where survey forms were sent to the traffic engineering agency. In a few cities the effectiveness of the controls is perceived as poor. The number of cities reporting each effectiveness rating is given in Table 8.

TABLE 8

PERCEIVED EFFECTIVENESS OF LOCAL BUS STOP TRAFFIC CONTROLS (Number of Cities)

| | Perceived Effectiveness | | |
|---|---|---|---|
| Population Group | Good | Fair | Poor |
| 50,000 - 100,000 | 20 | 9 | 0 |
| 100,000 - 250,000 | 29 | 5 | 2 |
| 250,000 - 1,000,000 | 19 | 6 | 2 |
| All groups | 68 | 20 | 4 |

### Need for Additional National Standards for Bus Stop Traffic Controls

The national standards of the MUTCD for the use of traffic control devices to control parking at bus stops are given in Appendix A and discussed earlier in the synthesis. These were last revised in 1978.

Thirty-six percent of the 92 respondents to the survey sent to traffic engineering agencies indicated that they thought there was a need for additional national standards for the use of traffic control devices to control parking at bus stops. Table 9, however, shows that the perceived need for additional standards was greatest in cities with populations between 50,000 and 100,000.

There is some correlation between the perceived need for additional national standards and the respondents' evaluation of the effectiveness of their local bus stop parking controls. More cities that rated the effectiveness of their local controls as fair or poor indicated a need for additional standards than did cities that rated their local controls as good. The correlation, shown in Table 10, is limited.

## USE OF NO PARKING SIGNS AND CURB MARKINGS IN OTHER JURISDICTIONS

A limited amount of information on the use of parking prohibition signs and curb markings was collected from multi-jurisdiction transit districts and cities with populations under 50,000 and over 1,000,000. The information, although limited, indicates that in those districts and cities there also is diversi-

TABLE 7

AGENCY RESPONSIBLE FOR BUS STOP SIGNS AND CURB MARKINGS (Percent of 137 Cities in Study Survey)

| Agency | Bus Stop Location Sign | Parking Prohibition Signs and Curb Markings |
|---|---|---|
| Traffic Engineering or Public Works | 46 | 93 |
| Transit | 49 | 5 |
| Transit and Traffic Engineering or Public Works | 5 | 2 |

TABLE 9

NUMBER OF CITIES PERCEIVING A NEED FOR ADDITIONAL NATIONAL STANDARDS FOR BUS STOP TRAFFIC CONTROLS

| Population Group | Perceive A Need | Do Not Perceive A Need |
|---|---|---|
| 50,000 - 100,000 | 16 | 12 |
| 100,000 - 250,000 | 9 | 26 |
| 250,000 - 1,000,000 | 8 | 19 |
| All groups | 33 | 57 |

TABLE 10

PERCEIVED EFFECTIVENESS OF LOCAL BUS STOP TRAFFIC CONTROLS AND NEED FOR ADDITIONAL NATIONAL STANDARDS (Number of Cities)

| Perceived Effectiveness of Local Controls | Perceived Need for Additional National Standards | |
|---|---|---|
| | Yes | No |
| Good | 21 | 45 |
| Fair | 10 | 10 |
| Poor | 2 | 2 |

fication in the types of signs and curb markings used and the patterns of use.

### Cities Over 1,000,000

Four of the five cities with populations over 1,000,000 responding to the survey have parking prohibition traffic controls at all bus stops. Two use only signs, and two use curb markings at all stops with supplemental signs at problem locations. The fifth city uses parking prohibition signs only at bus stops in the central business district and at a limited number of problem locations outside that area. The types of signs, colors of curb markings used, and the pattern of their use are given in Table 11.

### Cities Under 50,000

The 14 cities under 50,000 population responding to the survey use most of the parking prohibition traffic controls for bus stops with the same diversity shown in larger cities. None of the cities were in states where red curb markings are in general use. That geographic limitation in the sample may be why none of the cities reported using red curb markings. Table 12 gives the extent to which the various devices are used in those cities and the patterns of their use.

### Transit Districts

Survey forms were returned by 28 transit districts that operate in multi-jurisdiction, urban-suburban-rural areas. The districts range in size from large, 2500-vehicle fleet operations to small agencies operating as few as 10 buses. These districts were in 14 states.

The use of bus stop parking prohibition signs and curb markings in the areas served by these agencies is as diversified as the use in cities with populations between 50,000 and 1,000,000. The same types of signs, colors of curb markings, and patterns of control are used. The extent to which they are used is given in Table 13.

Most transit districts have reasonable uniformity in the use of signs and curb markings over the entire system. Some, however, reported that they could not get all the jurisdictions they

TABLE 12

USE OF BUS STOP TRAFFIC CONTROL DEVICES IN CITIES WITH POPULATION OF LESS THAN 50,000 (14 Cities)

| Control Device Use | Number of Cities |
|---|---|
| Signs | |
| Type A | 6 |
| Type B | 2 |
| Type C | 6 |
| Curb Markings | |
| Yellow | 10 |
| Red | - |
| Other | 1 |
| Patterns of Use | |
| Signs only | 3 |
| Curb markings only | - |
| Signs and curb markings | 11 |
| No traffic control devices | - |

TABLE 11

USE OF BUS STOP TRAFFIC CONTROL DEVICES IN CITIES WITH POPULATION OF MORE THAN 1,000,000 (5 Cities)

| Control Device Use | Number of Cities |
|---|---|
| Signs | |
| Type A | 1 |
| Type B | 4 |
| Type C | - |
| Curb Markings | |
| Yellow | - |
| Red | 2 |
| Other | - |
| Patterns of Use | |
| Signs only | 3 |
| Curb markings only | - |
| Signs and curb markings | 2 |
| No traffic control devices | - |

TABLE 13

USE OF BUS STOP TRAFFIC CONTROL DEVICES BY TRANSIT DISTRICTS (28 Districts)

| Control Device Use | Number of Districts |
|---|---|
| Signs | |
| Type A | 8 |
| Type B | 2 |
| Type C | 9 |
| Curb Markings | |
| Yellow | 10 |
| Red | 6 |
| Other | 1 |
| Patterns of Use | |
| Signs only | 7 |
| Curb markings only | 5 |
| Signs and curb markings | 12 |
| No traffic control devices | 4 |

serve to use the same system of signs and/or curb markings. In the survey, those districts reported the devices used in the majority of the jurisdictions they serve.

### OTHER CURB LANE TRAFFIC CONTROLS AT BUS STOPS

Curb lane traffic controls, such as all-day or peak-hour parking prohibitions and bus-only and high-occupancy-vehicle regulations, generally improve bus operations and create no problems at bus stops. Right-turn-only lanes at signalized intersections and reserved, marked bicycle lanes at the curb—a Class II Bikeway—can create safety and operating problems for buses, turning vehicles, and bicycles. Those problems are solved by good planning. Traffic engineering and transit agencies determine acceptable alternative mid-block or far-side locations instead of near-side stops where right-turn lanes are proposed. In the case of Class II Bikeways, the problem should be dealt with in the planning process by not locating that type of bikeway on bus-route streets. One author has written: "Bikeways along streets with bus routes present a problem to bicycles and buses . . ." (*6*). On a bus-route street a Class II Bikeway cannot be a continuous, exclusive right-of-way for bicycles. The lane can be occupied by buses loading or discharging passengers.

CHAPTER THREE

# CONCLUSIONS AND RECOMMENDATIONS

Parking regulation and control at urban transit bus stops in the United States is done in a number of ways. Cities follow one of four different concepts for the use of controls and control devices.

- The same type of signs and/or curb markings are used at all stops.
- All stops have the same basic pattern of signs and/or curb markings, and supplemental signs and/or curb markings are used at selected stops.
- Parking controls are used only as needed, and signs and/or curb markings are used only at selected stops or groups of stops.
- Parking prohibition signs and/or curb markings are not used at bus stops.

Three types of No Parking signs and a variety of curb markings, alone or in combination, are used to indicate the parking prohibition when one is established. In this study, 54 different use patterns of those devices were identified.

Most of the signs and curb markings that are used conform to the standards of the MUTCD. The one exception is the combined Bus Stop Location-No Parking sign, R7-107a in the MUTCD. Twenty percent of the cities using that type of sign have a local design that is substantially different from the MUTCD design.

The diversity in the types of traffic control devices used and their application at bus stops apparently does not impair their effectiveness. In 92 cities with populations over 50,000, very few city officials rated the effectiveness of their local bus stop parking controls as poor, and more than half rated their local controls as good. Officials in 33 of those cities perceived a need for additional national standards or guidelines for the signs and curb markings used at bus stops.

In response to perceived needs identified in the study, research is recommended on two aspects of parking controls at bus stops:

1. Additional or revised national standards for the signs and curb markings that are used for parking prohibitions, including providing more flexibility in the design standards for the combined Bus Stop Location-No Parking sign.
2. Guidelines on when parking controls should be established at bus stops, including determination of the need for additional controls at selected or special locations, such as median transit stops and contra-flow lanes.

The research should evaluate the validity of the perceived need, and, if appropriate, develop guidelines or proposed standards.

# REFERENCES

1. U.S. Department of Transportation, Federal Highway Administration, *Manual on Uniform Traffic Control Devices.* Superintendent of Documents, U.S. Government Printing Office, Washington, D.C. 20402 (1978).
2. Transportation Research Board, *Glossary of Urban Public Transportation Terms,* Special Report 179, National Research Council, Washington, D.C. (1978).
3. American Public Transit Association, *On-Street Information,* American Public Transit Association, 1225 Connecticut Avenue, N.W., Washington, D.C. 20036.
4. National Committee on Uniform Traffic Laws and Ordinances, *Model Traffic Ordinance,* National Committee on Uniform Traffic Laws and Ordinances, 555 Clark Street, P.O. Box 1409, Evanston, Illinois 60204.
5. Institute of Transportation Engineers, *A Recommended Practice for Proper Location of Bus Stops,* Institute of Transportation Engineers, 525 School Street S.W., Washington, D.C. 20024.
6. Federal Highway Administration, *Environmental Analysis and Citizen Participation,* National Technical Information Service, Springfield, Va. 22151.

# APPENDIX A

## EXCERPTS FROM MODEL TRAFFIC ORDINANCE

Section 15-5

City traffic engineer* to designate public carrier stops and stands

The city traffic engineer is hereby authorized and required to establish bus stops . . . on such public streets in such places and in such number as he shall determine to be of the greatest benefit and convenience to the public, and every such bus stop . . . shall be designated by appropriate signs.

Section 15-7**

Restricted use of bus and taxicab stands

No person shall stop, stand or park a vehicle other than a bus in a bus stop . . . when any such stop . . . has been officially designated and appropriately signed, except that the driver of a passenger vehicle may temporarily stop therein for the purpose of and while actually engaged in loading or unloading passengers when such stopping does not interfere with any bus . . . waiting to enter or about to enter such zone.

* Section 2-10 of the MTO designates that the city engineer shall serve as the city traffic engineer if a city has no city traffic engineer.

** Ordinance may be written to prohibit stopping, standing, or parking.

# APPENDIX B

## EXCERPTS FROM MANUAL ON UNIFORM TRAFFIC CONTROL DEVICES

### 2B-31 Urban Parking and Stopping Signs (R7 Series)

. . . Generally, parking signs should display such of the following information as is appropriate, from top to bottom of the sign, in the order listed:

1. Restriction or prohibition.
2. Time of day it is applicable, if not at all hours.
3. Days of week applicable, if not every day.

In addition there should be a single-headed arrow pointing in the direction the regulation is in effect, if the sign is at the end of a zone, or a double-headed arrow pointing both ways, if the sign is at an intermediate point in a zone. As an alternate to the arrow, if the signs are posted facing traffic at an angle of 90 degrees to the curb line, there may be included on the sign, or on a separate plate below the sign, such legend as BEGIN, END, HERE TO CORNER . . . .

Where parking is prohibited at all times or at specified times, parking signs shall have red letters and border on a white background . . . .

Alternate designs for the R7-107 sign are permissible (R7-107a). Alternate designs may include, on a single panel, a transit logo, an approved bus symbol, a parking prohibition, the words BUS STOP, and an arrow. The preferred bus symbol color is black but other dark colors may be used. Additionally, the transit logo may be shown on the bus face in the appropriate colors in lieu of placing the logo separately. The reverse side of the sign may contain bus routing information . . . .

The words NO PARKING may be used as an alternative to the No Parking symbol . . . on sign . . . R7-107a.

### 2B-32 Placement of Urban Parking Signs

When parking signs with arrows are used to indicate the extent of the restricted zones, the signs should be set at an angle of not less than 30 nor more than 45 degrees with the line of traffic flow to be visible to approaching traffic.

Care should be exercised to see that the single arrows point in the proper direction to indicate the regulated zone. Where the zone is unusually long, signs showing a double arrow are desirable at intermediate points within the zone.

If the signs are mounted at an angle of 90 degrees to the curb line, two signs shall be mounted back to back at the transition point between two parking zones, each with the appended plate reading THIS SIDE OF SIGN. At intermediate points within a zone, a single sign without any arrow or appended plate should be used, facing in the direction of approaching traffic. Otherwise the standards of placement should be the same as for signs using directional arrows.

### 3B-18 Curb Markings for Parking Restrictions

Since curb markings of yellow and white are used for delineation and visibility, it is usually advisable to establish parking regulations through the installation of standard signs (secs. 2B-31 to 33). However, when local authorities prescribe special colors for curb markings as supplemental to standard signs, they may be used.

When signs are not used, intended meaning should be stenciled on the curb.

Signs shall always be used with curb markings in those areas where curb markings are frequently obliterated by accumulations of snow and ice.

# APPENDIX C

## SURVEY FORMS

SURVEY FORM A (Distributed to city traffic engineers)

SURVEY OF TRAFFIC CONTROLS AT BUS STOPS

1. Is parking in bus stops prohibited by local law or ordinance?

   ____ Yes

   ____ No

2. Is a No Parking legend incorporated into the bus stop location sign?

   ____ Yes

   ____ No (if no, go to question 3)

   If yes:

   a. Which sign best resembles the type used:

      ____ A
      ____ B
      ____ Other - Please furnish a photo or sketch

A

B

   b. Where is this type of sign used?

      Check one

      ____ At all stops

      ____ Routinely in areas with high parking demand

      ____ Only at problem locations

c. If this type of sign is not used at all stops, who determines the locations where it will be used?

______________________________________________________________

______________________________________________________________

d. If there are written policies for the use of this sign, please furnish a copy.

3. When a no parking legend is not incorporated into the bus stop location sign:

a. Are separate No Parking signs used in conjunction with the bus stop location sign?

Check one

____ No

____ At all stops

____ Routinely in areas with high parking demand

____ Only at problem locations

b. If a separate No Parking sign is not used at all bus stops who determines where they will be used?

______________________________________________________________

______________________________________________________________

c. If there is a policy on this use of No Parking signs, please furnish a copy.

4. Additional No Parking signs at bus stops

a. Are additional No Parking signs used to mark the limits of the bus stop parking prohibition?

Check uses

| Stop Location | | | |
|---|---|---|---|
| Near Side | Far Side | Mid-Block | |
| ____ | ____ | ____ | No |
| ____ | ____ | ____ | Routinely in areas of high parking demand |
| ____ | ____ | ____ | Only at problem locations |

b. If this use of No Parking signs is not used at all stops, who determines the locations where they will be used?

________________________________________________

________________________________________________

c. If there is a policy on this use of No Parking signs, please furnish a copy.

d. If No Parking signs are used to mark the limits of the parking prohibition at bus stops, please note normal length of the prohibition on the bus stop diagrams shown below.

Location of No Parking Signs at Bus Stops

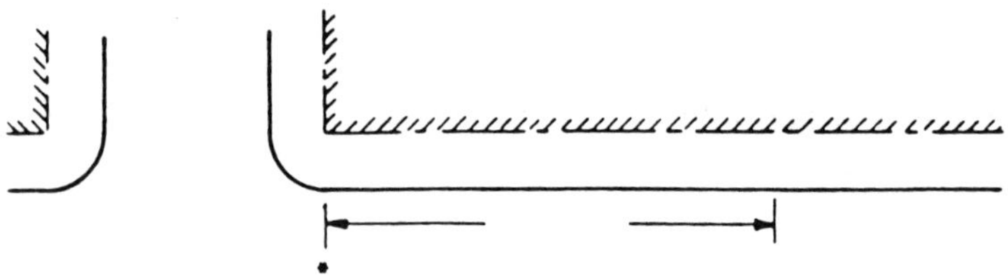

NORMAL NEAR-SIDE BUS STOP

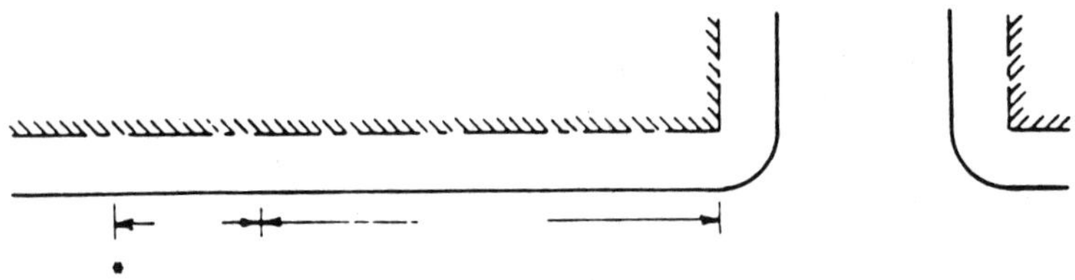

NORMAL FAR-SIDE BUS STOP

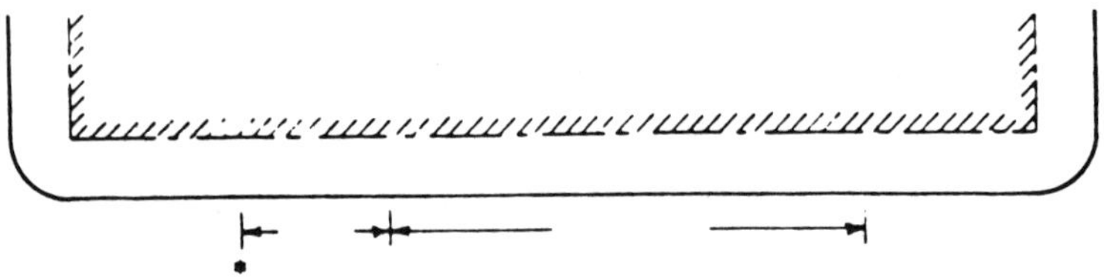

NORMAL MID-BLOCK BUS STOP

• Bus stop location sign

5. Are curb markings used to indicate no parking in bus stops?

   Check one

   ____ No

   ____ At all stops

   ____ Routinely in areas with high parking demand

   ____ Only at problem locations

6. If curb markings are used, what color are they?

   ______________________________________________________________

7. Where curb markings are used, are signs also used to mark the parking prohibition?

   Check one

   ____ No

   ____ At all locations

   ____ Routinely in areas with high parking demand

   ____ Only at problem locations

8. Who is responsible for the erection and maintenance of:

   a. Bus stop location signs

   b. No Parking signs at bus stops

   c. Curb markings at bus stops

9. How would you rate the effectiveness of bus stop parking prohibition controls in your city?

   Check one

   ____ Good

   ____ Fair

   ____ Poor

10. Do you think there is a need for national standards for the use of traffic control devices to control parking at bus stops? (In addition to those in the Manual On Uniform Traffic Control Devices)

____ Yes

____ No

11. Do you have any special traffic controls at bus stops? If so, please describe.

____________________

____________________

____________________

____________________

12. Other comments on traffic control at bus stops.

____________________

____________________

____________________

____________________

____________________

Thank you for your cooperation

SURVEY FORM B (Distributed to transit system personnel)

## SURVEY OF TRAFFIC CONTROLS IN BUS STOPS

1. Is parking in bus stops prohibited by local law or ordinance?

____ Yes

____ No

2. Is a No Parking legend incorporated into the bus stop location sign?

____ Yes

____ No (if no, go to question 3)

If yes:

a. Which sign best resembles the type used?

____ A

____ B

A

B

b. Are additional No Parking signs used to mark the limits of the bus stop?

Check one

____ No

____ At all stops

____ Routinely in areas with high parking demand

____ Only at problem locations

3. When a No Parking legend is not incorporated into the bus stop location sign:

   a. Are separate No Parking signs used in conjunction with the bus stop location sign?

      Check one

      ____ No

      ____ At all stops

      ____ Routinely in areas with high parking demand

      ____ Only at problem locations

   b. Are additional No Parking signs used to mark the limits of the bus stop?

      Check one

      ____ No

      ____ At all stops

      ____ Routinely in areas with high parking demand

      ____ Only at problem locations

4. Are curb markings used to indicate no parking in bus stops?

   Check one

   ____ No

   ____ At all stops

   ____ Routinely in areas with high parking demand

   ____ Only at problem locations

5. If curb markings are used, what color are they?

   ______________________________

6. Who is responsible for the erection and maintenance of:

   Bus stop location signs ______________________________

   No parking signs and curb markings ______________________________

7. Other comments on traffic and parking controls at bus stops.

# APPENDIX D

## SURVEY RESPONDENTS

CITIES WITH POPULATION OF 250,000 TO 1,000,000

ALABAMA
Birmingham

ARIZONA
Phoenix

CALIFORNIA
Long Beach
Oakland
Sacramento
San Diego
San Francisco
San Jose

COLORADO
Denver

DISTRICT OF COLUMBIA

FLORIDA
Jacksonville
Miami-Dade
Tampa

INDIANA
Indianapolis

KANSAS
Wichita

KENTUCKY
Louisville

LOUISIANA
New Orleans

MARYLAND
Baltimore

MINNESOTA
St. Paul

MISSOURI
Kansas City

NEBRASKA
Omaha

NEW MEXICO
Albuquerque

NEW YORK
Buffalo

NORTH CAROLINA
Charlotte

OHIO
Cleveland
Columbus
Toledo

OKLAHOMA
Oklahoma City
Tulsa

OREGON
Portland

PENNSYLVANIA
Pittsburgh

TENNESSEE
Memphis

TEXAS
Austin
Dallas
El Paso
Fort Worth
San Antonio

VIRGINIA
Norfolk

WASHINGTON
Seattle

WISCONSIN
Milwaukee

CITIES WITH POPULATION OF LESS THAN 50,000

ALASKA
Juneau

IOWA
Ames

LOUISIANA
Gretna

MINNESOTA
St. Cloud

NEW JERSEY
Atlantic City

NEW YORK
Ithaca

NORTH CAROLINA
Chapel Hill
Wilson

OHIO
Zanesville

VIRGINIA
Blacksburg

WASHINGTON
Port Angeles
Raymond
Walla Walla

WISCONSIN
Oskosh

CITIES WITH POPULATION MORE THAN 1,000,000

CALIFORNIA
Los Angeles

ILLINOIS
Chicago

NEW YORK
New York

PENNSYLVANIA
Philadelphia

TEXAS
Houston

TRANSIT DISTRICTS (Central Office City)

CALIFORNIA
Antioch
Arcata
Garden Grove
Monterey
Palm Springs
San Rafael

FLORIDA
Fort Lauderdale
Melbourne
Sarasota
West Palm Beach

HAWAII
Hilo

IDAHO
Coeur d'Alene

KENTUCKY
Fort Wright

MASSACHUSETTS
Amherst

MICHIGAN
Bay City
Detroit

NEW JERSEY
Maplewood

NEW YORK
East Meadow

OHIO
Lima

OREGON
Medford

PENNSYLVANIA
East Stroudsburg
Johnstown
Kingston
Pottsville

SOUTH CAROLINA
Florence

WASHINGTON
Lynnwood
Olympia

## CITIES WITH POPULATION OF 50,000 TO 100,000

CALIFORNIA
- Fairfield
- Oceanside
- Orange
- Redwood City
- Santa Ana
- Santa Rosa
- Walnut Creek

COLORADO
- Boulder

GEORGIA
- Albany

ILLINOIS
- Aurora
- Decatur

INDIANA
- Bloomington

IOWA
- Council Bluffs
- Iowa City

KANSAS
- Overland Park

LOUISIANA
- Lafayette

MAINE
- Portland

MASSACHUSETTS
- Brockton
- Cambridge

MICHIGAN
- Dearborn
- Saginaw

MINNESOTA
- Duluth

MONTANA
- Billings

NEW YORK
- Troy

NORTH CAROLINA
- High Point

OHIO
- Hamilton

OREGON
- Salem

PENNSYLVANIA
- Altoona
- Lancaster

RHODE ISLAND
- East Providence

SOUTH CAROLINA
- Charleston
- Greenville

SOUTH DAKOTA
- Sioux Falls

TEXAS
- Abilene

VIRGINIA
- Lynchburg
- Roanoke

WASHINGTON
- Vancouver
- Yakima

WEST VIRGINIA
- Huntington

WISCONSIN
- Appleton
- Janesville
- Racine

WYOMING
- Casper

## CITIES WITH POPULATION OF 100,000 TO 250,000

ALASKA
- Anchorage

ARIZONA
- Tempe

ARKANSAS
- Little Rock

CALIFORNIA
- Anaheim
- Bakersfield
- Fresno
- Modesto
- Oxnard
- Riverside

COLORADO
- Lakewood
- Pueblo

CONNECTICUT
- Bridgeport
- Hartford
- New Haven

FLORIDA
- St. Petersburg

GEORGIA
- Savannah

ILLINOIS
- Peoria
- Rockford
- Springfield

IOWA
- Cedar Rapids
- Des Moines

KANSAS
- Topeka

MASSACHUSETTS
- Worcester

MICHIGAN
- Flint
- Grand Rapids
- Lansing

MISSISSIPPI
- Jackson

MISSOURI
- Springfield

NEBRASKA
- Lincoln

NEVADA
- Las Vegas
- Reno

NEW YORK
- Rochester
- Syracuse

NORTH CAROLINA
- Greensboro
- Raleigh
- Winston-Salem

OHIO
- Akron
- Dayton

OREGON
- Eugene

PENNSYLVANIA
- Allentown
- Erie

RHODE ISLAND
- Providence

TENNESSEE
- Chattanooga
- Knoxville

TEXAS
- Amarillo
- Beaumont
- Waco

UTAH
- Salt Lake City

VIRGINIA
- Newport News
- Richmond

WASHINGTON
- Spokane
- Tacoma

WISCONSIN
- Madison

# APPENDIX E

## SUBPATTERNS OF USES OF BUS STOP CONTROL DEVICES

| Sign Type & Use[b] | Curb Markings - Use and Color[a] | | | | | | |
|---|---|---|---|---|---|---|---|
| | | All Stops | | | Selected Stops | | |
| | None | Y | R | O | Y | R | O |
| **One sign - all stops** | | | | | | | |
| A | 9 | 2 | - | - | 2 | 1 | - |
| B | - | 1 | - | - | 1 | - | - |
| A & B | 1 | - | - | 1 | 1 | - | - |
| C | 1 | - | - | - | - | - | - |
| **Two or more signs - all stops** | | | | | | | |
| A | 2 | - | - | - | - | - | - |
| B | 1 | - | - | - | 1 | - | - |
| A & B | - | - | - | - | - | - | - |
| C | 1 | - | - | - | 1 | - | - |
| **One sign - all stops; and one or more - selected stops** | | | | | | | |
| A | 6 | - | - | - | 1 | 2 | 1 |
| B | 2 | - | - | - | 1 | - | - |
| A & B | 2 | - | - | - | - | - | - |
| C | 2 | - | - | - | - | - | - |
| **One sign - selected stops** | | | | | | | |
| A | 2 | - | - | - | 1 | 2 | - |
| B | 5 | - | 1 | - | 5 | - | - |
| A & B | - | - | - | - | 1 | - | 1 |
| c | 5 | 1 | - | - | 3 | 2 | - |
| **Two or more signs - selected stops** | | | | | | | |
| A | 1 | - | - | - | 2 | 1 | 2 |
| B | 10 | - | - | - | 1 | 1 | 1 |
| A & B | - | - | - | - | 2 | - | - |
| C | 9 | 1 | 1 | - | 8 | 6 | 1 |
| No signs | 9 | - | 2 | - | 1 | 6 | - |

[a] Y = yellow; R = red; O = other

[b] Sign at the bus loading point.

# APPENDIX F

## BUS STOPS IN THROUGH-TRAFFIC LANES*

INTRODUCTION

The subject of bus stops in though-traffic lanes was noted in the project scope, but was not covered in the report. Subsequently, a survey was sent to 43 large transit operators in the United States and Canada. The operators are in major metropolitan areas that have heavily traveled arterials with transit service. Responses were received from 25 of the operators, a 58 percent return.

FINDINGS

Although there is a widespread use of bus stops in through-traffic lanes, the transit operators have not experienced any significant traffic safety problems, and, therefore, have not had a need to look for any new or special traffic control signs or pavement markings.

The following is a summary of the questionnaire responses.

1. Bus stops on a through lane on an arterial without shoulders or curb parking. When a bus stops it blocks the lane for following vehicles.

A. Does this type of bus stop exist in your service area?

All respondents have bus stops in through-traffic lanes.

B. If you have any accident problems, please describe.

Rear-end accidents are the typical problem, but in no case was it identified as a serious or major problem.

C. If you have any operational problems, please describe.

Typical operational problem was vehicles being parked in the through lane. This has been identified as an enforcement problem.

D. If any special signs or pavement markings are used to improve safety or operational problems, please describe.

In general, only the standard bus stop sign and curb painting were used. Any additional signs or markings were a rare exception.

2. Bus stops on an arterial where parking is prohibited during peak hours and the curb lane becomes a through lane.

A. Does this type of bus stop exist in your service area?

Twenty-one of the 25 respondents reported that they operated next to the curb as a through lane when there were peak hour parking prohibitions.

---

* By Charles E. Zell; Transportation Engineer, Sacramento, California.

B. If you have any accident or operational problems, please describe.

The typical operating problem was illegal parking, not traffic safety.

C. If any special signs or pavement markings are used to improve safety or operational problems, please describe.

Several operators noted that the curb lane is marked as an exclusive bus or HOV lane for peak periods.

3. Near-side bus stops in designated or marked right-turn lanes.

A. Do you have any bus stops in right-turn lanes?

Only four operators reported that they did not have a near-side bus stop in a right-turn lane. The near-side bus stop problem generated 34 comments for questions 3 A through E. This is more than twice the number for either question 1 or 2.

B. If you have any accident or operational problems with right-turning vehicles turning in front of a stopped bus, please describe.

There was a consensus that the near-side stop in a right-turn lane is undesirable and should be avoided when traffic volumes create a problem. One operator reported a problem for the far-side stop alternative in that following vehicles do not expect the bus to stop again when it stopped for a traffic signal. Several operators reported a minor problem of vehicles turning in front of the bus from the adjacent lane. There was a consensus that driver training is important so that the driver will be alert for such turning vehicles.

C. If you have any operational problems with right-turning vehicles blocking the bus stop, please describe.

Seven operators commented on problems of right-turning vehicles blocking the bus stop.

D. If a traffic sign is used to exempt the bus from the required right turn, please describe.

Nearly half of the operators noted the use of "Except Buses" panel when "Right Lane Must Turn Right" sign is used. However, there were some variations on the design of the sign and the use of the exception panel.

E. If any traffic signs or pavement markings are used to restrict the right turn from the second lane from the curb, please describe.

A straight arrow pavement marking in the lane adjacent to the right turn and bus stop lane was noted to be effective.

4. If you have bus stops in other unique or problem places, please describe.

   Several unique problems were noted with bus stops. Tee intersections were reported as a problem. Bus stops near freeway on-ramps are a problem when the ramp is metered. Far-side bus stops in front of driveways have a conflict with vehicles turning into the driveway. Certain types of businesses adjacent to the bus stop create some problems, but this may be more of an enforcement problem than one of signing. One operator has bus stops in the median, and buses have difficulty returning to the through lane. Shopping malls and high bridges were reported as problem areas by one operator.

## CONCLUSIONS

Rear-end accidents are not a general problem when buses stop in a through-traffic lane, although there may be a need for advance warning signs for bus stops in a through lane when such stops are infrequent. An advance warning sign for a bus stop in a through-traffic lane should be developed and tested for its effectiveness. Pavement markings may provide some warning, but they lose their effectiveness as the density of traffic increases.

Rear-end accidents have been reduced during demonstrations of eye-level, center-mounted brake lights. The effectiveness of such lights has resulted in a revision of the Federal Motor Vehicle Safety Standards to require the lights on new passenger cars. Eye-level, center-mounted brake lights should be tested on transit buses to evaluate their effectiveness in reducing rear-end accidents.

The extensive use of "Except Buses" sign panel would justify the establishment of such a sign in the Manual of Uniform Traffic Control Devices.

The only unique bus stop location problem that may justify further study is the Tee intersection.